Moonlight silence

by
Nasreen Latif

BlueRose ONE.com
Stories Matter
NewDelhi • London

BLUEROSE PUBLISHERS
India | U.K.

For permissions requests or inquiries regarding this publication, please contact:

BLUEROSE PUBLISHERS
www.BlueRoseONE.com
info@bluerosepublishers.com
+91 8882 898 898
+4407342408967

ISBN: 978-93-6452-075-1

Cover Design: Saher Malik
Typesetting: Pooja Sharma

First Edition: February 2025

MOONLIGHT SILENCE

Biography

At a tender age I started writing Poetry as a hobby and rather a soothing addiction to my Soul...

It became an everyday habit writing a Poem on daily basis, especially during Twilight hours, as it was an antidote to a good Night's sleep, often giving me deep satisfaction, whenever I penned a new Poem and I would SMILE to myself.

My true essence of writing Poetry is, 'Am an essence of myself', a reminder of me, my circumstances that evolved into thoughts...

There is no set rule I follow, though I enjoy writing Haikus and freestyle Poems...

I can choose any topic...May it be Pain, Laughter, Love, Suicide, Nature, that would make me pen a Poem instantly, the list is endless ...

Poetry surely is fascinating! Every word I choose to write, there is always a deep hidden meaning behind it. Like the setting or rising of the Sun, bringing along a new beginning or ending. Such is my story enveloped into a burst of emotions turning into poems!

Explaining a lonely Soul is like a dried creeper with a single Leaf hanging on to dear life, not knowing when the end would be nigh!

I have carefully chosen the Poems for this Anthology...Each one a 'Whisper from my Soul'...Words that are based entirely on my thoughts and feelings to bring awareness to life's true meaning...

Pain has been a greater part of me, of which a lot of my thoughts are based on, in my Poems...

Looking around me in search of answers about life's true meaning, Wars have taken over innocent lives, leaving thousands homeless, hungry and every Soul inflicted by despair... There is so much Pain around the World, That surely one wonders if there is a future for future generations!

Am torn between the thought that a 'Mother is carrying her innocent Child in her Arms and it's lifeless! 'Ohh World open your Eyes' feel the Pain!

Poetry is the voice of the Soul, bringing light into Darkness like lighting a Candle in a dark room. The Shadows on the Walls painting a picture .

As the Moonlight shines thru a Window, there is a strange silence that always follows, mysterious and creepy...Arousing emotions that turn thoughts into Words on Paper! Such is the power of the Moon... My Soul too glows at the sight of a full moon just like silence of the outbound Waves of the Sea...A soothing experience, just the symphonies of the Breeze calming the Soul...

My dedication goes to Saher Malik

♡♡♡♡♡♡♡♡♡

The Essence of my Love

My dear Child

The Rainbow that brings colour to my Life

The Sunrise after every Dawn

The Whisper at Dusk

The Red Rose in my Garden

♡◇♡◇♡◇♡◇♡◇

Contents

OHH AFRICA

As the Sun rises from the East
A lone Warrior paddling away his Canoe
In search of his catch for the Day

~nasreen

WHISPERS

Under the Whispers of the Trees
Deep love blossomed

Two young Hearts
Enthralled by each other

A running River
Under their Boat

Making tiny Whirlpools
Wherever their Hands would touch

In harmony with Nature
Love Hearts singing

Birds breaking the occasional silence by chirping
The Boat gliding downstream...

~nasreen

NATURE'S LIGHTS

A beautiful Night
Alone in my backyard

Under the Canopy of Trees
As I walk around my Garden...

Tiny little Lamps
Lighting my path

Am mesmerised
Fire flies playing hide and seek amongst the Bushes

~nasreen

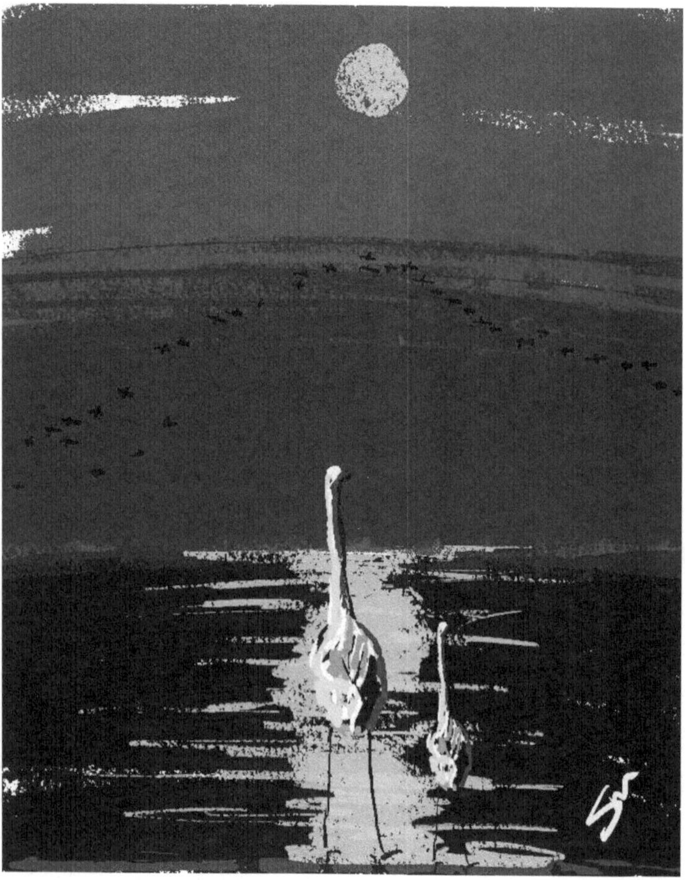

THE LAST HERON

Moonlight over the Marshes
A lonely Heron on the Bank
The Flock migrating East

~nasreen

MIND'S EYE

A strange phenomenon
Clouds circling a blazing Sun
A Giant Vortex

~nasreen

THE WEE HOURS

Destruction in the wee hours
Surely Mankind how will you survive...?

When there are no Trees left
No Water catchments'

No Air to breathe
No Food

Just vast barren Land
Making me weep at sad old 'Mother Earth'

For a slow Death is creeping by the Day
Ice melting on the Snow covered regions

Floods spreading afar
Nothing but daily destruction

Hunger and despair looming
Disease and loss of lives

Ohh hear me World...!
Stop and think before it's too late

~nasreen

SPOOKY NIGHT

In the dark hours of a Moonlit Night
Silence in the old Streets

Sounds of Creepy Crawlies
A spooky Night

Owls cooing afar
Ready to pounce on a passing prey

Not a Soul in the Alleys
A disturbing scenario

Scaring my wits
Fear gripping me

Every step I turn to look around
Crackling Wind or is it Footsteps'

Ohhh... I hate this...!
My Footsteps gain momentum

~nasreen

MORNING DEW

Treading on soft morning Snow
The Crunch under my Feet somehow a Thriller

Grey Trees surrounding my Path
Ghostly appearances

My Heart starting to race
Am I the only one in the barren old Woods?

A canopy of Dew covered Branches
Hanging over...'

An occasional drip of Water from above
Making me stare at the Sky

A foggy morning it is...
A disturbing silence making me uncomfortable

~nasreen

UNDER THE MOON'S SHADOWS

Shadows playing under the Moon light
A dark creepy Night

Barren Trees swaying in the Blizzard
A cold Breeze whistling a Melody

Snow covered ground
A lone distant Wolf howling in the darkness

It's full Moon tonight
When the surroundings come to Life

~nasreen

SHADES OF GREY

As Winter persists
Snow laden Pine Trees stretching afar
At Dusk mistaking for Ghosts

~ nasreen

LUCID THOUGHTS

Seated forlorn in her own World
Sipping Wine and lost in her thoughts
Her loneliness a silent killer

~ nasreen

THE ORPHAN

A harsh reality in this Day and Age
A common scenario on the Streets

Hungry and desolate Children
No Parents

War-torn Zones on every corner of the Earth
Food a scarcity

Scavenging thru Dustbins
Torn Clothes and sullen faces

Hunger pangs driving the Little Ones to beg...!
No mercy from Heartless Humans'
Everyone running on their path
To an unforeseen future

A Bullet flies into a Child's Heart
A splutter of Blood

Down she drops to the ground
An unbearable site

Screams Echo in the Dusky Sky
Women moaning their Dead ones

Ohh miserable World!
Have mercy....Have mercy.....!

'For I lost a loved one...'
A Mother's plea...!

~nasreen

LUST

Under the warm bedding
Love blossomed into a Nightmare
A one Night Stand

~ nasreen

UNDER THE MOONLIGHT

Under the Shadows of the Moonlight
Boats gliding away in the silence of the Night
A beautiful scenario

~ nasreen

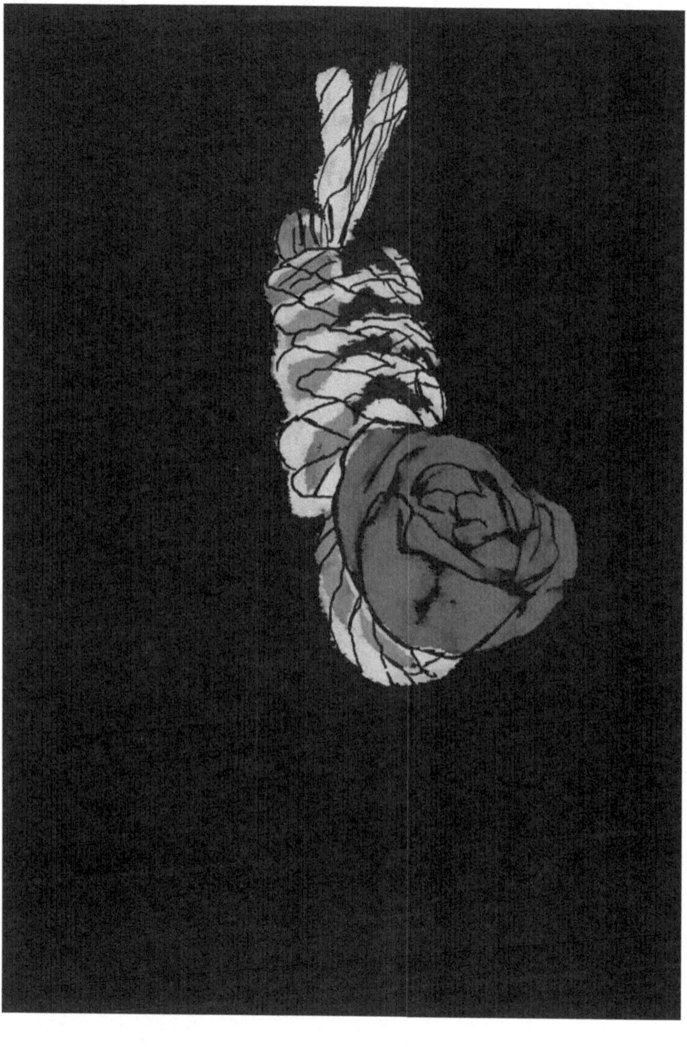

ROMANCE

Romance in Paris
Endless love
In a harmonious Tangle
I must have been bewitched by his presence
But Life had more for Me
One fine Day he walks away
Love strangled my Dreams

~nasreen

KNOCK KNOCK

A creepy Door in a secret hideout
Dusk bringing a strange Chill
Spooky Eyes follow my Footsteps

~nasreen

THE SAD TRUTH

A lonely Robin a visitor
Sad Memories of the unforgotten Soul
A flashback in my Mind

~ nasreen

BREATHTAKING MOONLIGHT

Magical Waves rolling in'
Breath-taking scenery

Enchanted atmosphere
Moonlight over the Sea

Shadows casted far beyond
Dolphins jumping in the Water

Hues of Purple and Grey
Align the beautiful evening Sky

Sea Breeze singing a Melody of the Oceans
The Water forming ripples

My Soul dancing to the Tune
'I can fly... I can fly'...

Time passes to Daylight
The Moon had cast a spell

~ nasreen

THE OLD WEDDING DRESS

Down in the Attic
An old Wedding Dress

Left to tell it's Tale
Still as beautiful

Though a bit dusty
And a few Cobwebs

Making me wonder who the Bride was
Years gone by...

Delicate Lace now ripping with my touch
Faded Colours of A sweet Memory

~nasreen

THE BURNING SAND

The Sahara Desert
Where there is no more existence

The Sand seems to have sucked all Lifeforms
A Rattle Snake crawling afar

A Scorpion ready to pounce
Dead Trees littering here and there

Once an Oasis
Now just a Nightmare

A frightening experience
A lone stranger amongst the Dead

Even the Breeze has ceased
Scorching Sunshine burning above

Walking the Giant Sand Dunes
There seems no end...

Desolate and worn
Thirst gets the better of me...

~nasreen

BRIDAL THOUGHTS

Sitting forlorn awaiting her Prince
Engulfed in thoughts of the unforeseen
Not sure of the future

~nasreen

THE LOST CARAVAN

Camels and Bedouin riders
Walking under the Desert Sunset

Orange hues covering the Skies
Dusk following immediately

Finally a cool Breeze
Tired and thirsty Nomads

In search of Green pastures for their Camels
Far beyond an Oasis... Or is it an illusion?

'Ooh look a Mirage'...
Endless walking

Darkness creeps in'
Yet no sign of Water

Thirsty Animals
Continuing to walk in search of the Life sustaining
source 'Water'

~nasreen

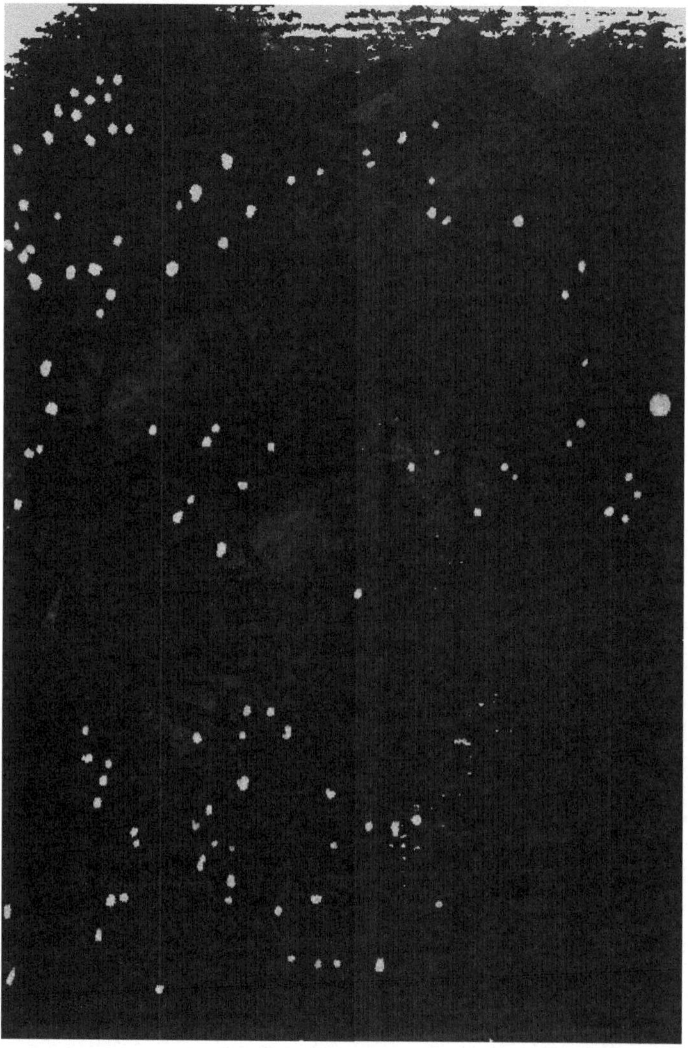

LONELINESS

Dew drops twinkling under the Moonlight
A single Maple Leaf
Reminding me of my loneliness

~nasreen

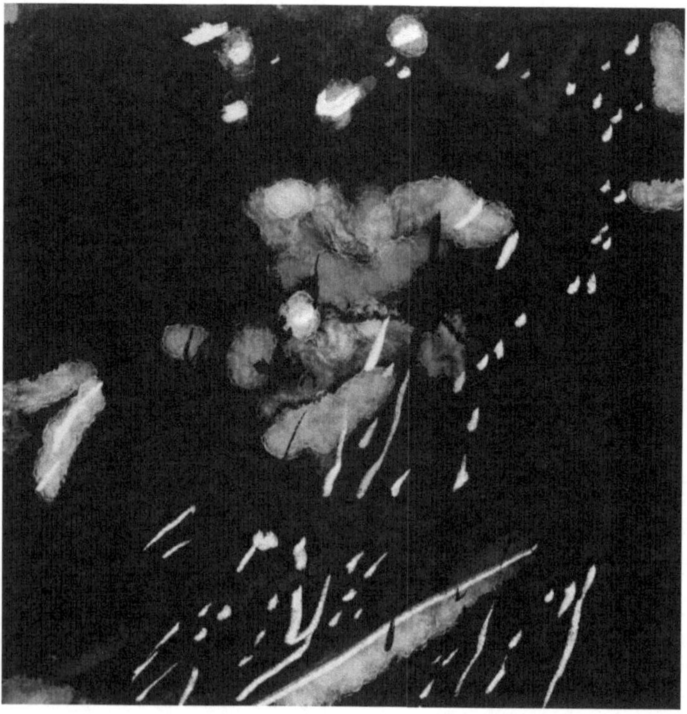

THE MIRROR

A noisy Street
Rain pouring

In the Dark Night
Am driving home

Street Lights a comfort
Am distracted

The Car's side Mirrors
My Memory Lane

Rain Drops running down the reflection
I forget am driving...

Distant thoughts clouding my Mind
My broken Life a turning point

Tears running down my cheeks
Now am just a lonely Soul

Sadness and Pain grips me
A deep void I see ahead

~nasreen

SHADOWS OF A CRESCENT MOON

Sitting on the edge of a Hill
A beautiful serene Night

My Mind is at Peace at the calmness
A Melodious Breeze surrounding me

The Crescent Moon appears in the dark Sky
And Twinkling Stars lighting up the Night

A mesmerizing scenario
Shadows of the Moonlight spreading afar

Deep in the Valley sounds of a running River
Silence broken by chirping Crickets

~nasreen

THE FORGOTTEN JETTY

Once a hub of activities
Fisherman bringing in their catch
Now just a resting ground for Seagulls

~nasreen

THE VILLAGE GIRL

A fair Maiden in all sense
Mesmerizing beauty from the East

Swaying on her way to the River
Making Heads turn...!

Ogling Eyes
Jeers and teasing

Tantalising movements as if seeking attention
The Men Folk whistling and shouting

Voila...! An attention seeker
Or just a Water bearer

~ nasreen

TURBULENCE

Turbulent Sea over the Mediterranean
Huge Waves rolling inland
Gushing back and forth in full strength

~ nasreen

LIFE'S MEANING

Today I blossom in all Glory
Yesterday I was just a Bud
Will I see a Tomorrow before I shrivel to nothing...?

~nasreen

TREASURES OF MY HEART

Loneliness from a broken Heart

My Diaries, a Memoir of my Love Life

He left without a Word

~nasreen

HELLO SPRING

Beautiful Daisies in full Blossoms
Spring bringing a splash of colour
Little knobs of Orange and White

~ nasreen

BEHIND THE VEIL

A hidden face
Behind the veil
Engulfed in her thoughts
A victim of Rape
Truth untold
Dwelling in pain and tears
Silenced from the World

~nasreen

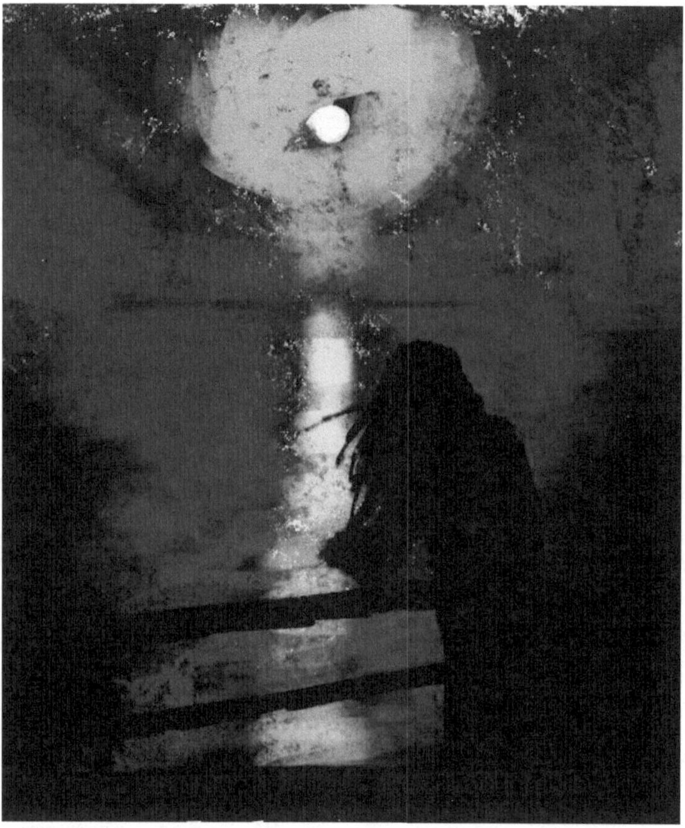

LONELY FIGURE

Mesmerising Moonlight over the Sea
A lonely figure on the Deck
Contemplating Suicide at Dusk

~nasreen

AS THE SUN SETS

A looming Dusk over the Horizon
Orange hues spreading afar

Blue Herons flying over the Lake
Heading South to their Nests

Sudden peace prevails
Am mesmerised by the scenery

In the silence Of the Wind
Suddenly the chorus of the creepy crawlies

Darkness setting in...
Time for me to head South too

~nasreen

UMBRELLAS

Calmness over the Sea
Floating umbrellas all over

Blinking my Eyes
Am floating in one, rocking me side to side

Am lost in my own World
A Nightmare or a Dream…?

Hearing whispers afar
A glowing light awakening me

~nasreen

THE SINGLE ROSE

Sleepless Nights
Forgotten dreams
He ripped my Heart
A forgotten love
Now appearing once more
'I don't want you'.... 'I don't.....!
Love is painful
Take away your lies
Broken promises
For they no longer hold prominence
Life must carry on
With or without you...!
My long forgotten love

~nasreen

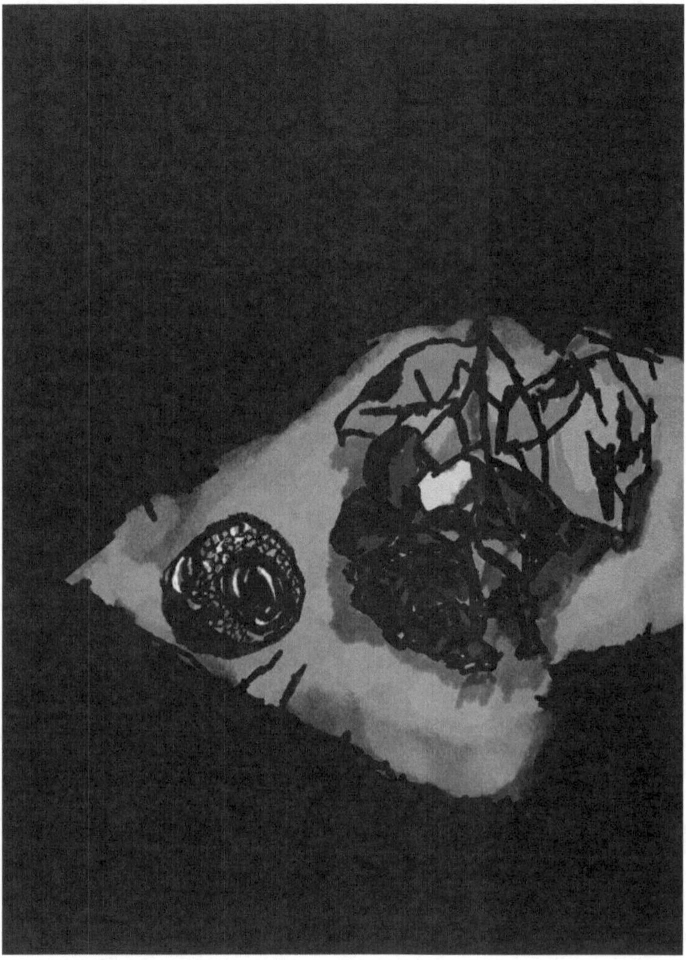

A THOUSAND WORDS

My Memoirs Of A Thousand Words
A reminder of my Love story

Every Page as if weeping
Tears of Blood

As desolate as I was
All Day looking out of the Window

My Knight in shining Armour
Would he ever come to take me from afar

I endured the Pain in my Heart
A Sapphire Ring a symbol of our Love

A reminder of a broken friendship
Now am left to count the Days

Every Dawn a new hope
Dusk arrives with sadness and Tears

~nasreen

SOUNDS OF NATURE

As the River cuts it's course
I marvel at the sound of the Water

Sitting on the edge of the Bank
Throwing Pebbles just to hear a 'Plonk'...

Each Pebble creating a ripple
Mind soothing'

Splashing Water as I walk in shallow Waters
Aaaahh.... Such calm feeling

The icy cold Water
Massaging my Feet as it runs down it's path

Endless chirping of the Birds
Sound of the Heron from afar

Such deep happiness engulfs my Soul
I finally find Peace

~nasreen

STRANDED

A lonely Boat washed away
Sitting alone on a Sandy Beach

Full Tide and not a single Soul around
Am left questioning my thoughts

A beautiful Sunny morning
Turquoise clear Waters

Calm Seas and hardly any Waves
Such scenic beauty surrounds me

All I find is a pair of Sandals
Could this be an answer to my questions

~nasreen

FARE THEE WELL

Sweet love
Fare thee well

Rain pouring and a cold Breeze
Surrounding them

Embracing his Love
'My love, 'He whispered'

'This Night is stormy'...
As their Lips touch

And so is my Heart'
'Tearing at my Ribs'...

A terrible Heartache
'Am leaving you now'...

Waving a goodbye
Not knowing if Fate would bring them back, together again

~nasreen

A NIGHT IN PARIS

A stormy Night in Paris
Gales and Thunderous Rain

Hiding under my Umbrella
Avoiding the downpour

A Taxi awaiting at the Street Corner
Not a Soul in sight

Scratching my Head
Now where to in this bewildering Night...?

~nasreen

TWILIGHT

Just as the Sun is crossing over the Horizon
A lonely Swan paddling home to Nest

Her shrill Quakes sounding loud and clear
Disturbing the serenity surrounding the Marshland

Her Cygnets hiding in the long Grass
Out of danger as the last Rays of the Sun disappear

A sudden calm spreads afar
No ripples in the cascading River

Time for a peaceful Night
As peace prevails over the Marshes

~nasreen

SECRETS OF THE DARK

A mesmerising Moonlight capturing me
Silence prevails yonder above a naked Tree

Stars twinkling bright
Singing the Melodies of a Moonlit Night

A whispering Breeze
Love the Night chill

Uhhhh... A warm hug would do...!
An Owl cooing in the distance

Suddenly taking flight over me
Maybe chasing a Bat or a Mouse

A slight shiver runs thru my Spine
A Spider spinning it's Web

The Cobweb shining in the glow of the Night
A sudden chirping under my Foot...

Scaring me outright
Time to go now...Enough of the Dark

~nasreen

A DASH OF SUNSHINE

Awakening at Dawn's first Rays
Different hues of Sunshine embracing me
What a delight Sunflowers are

~nasreen

SWEET LOVE

Intimate moments under the Shadows
A lone Candle burning a Romantic Flame
His caresses arousing her Passion

~nasreen

LIFE

Life blossomed on a lonely Path
Stardust making it Glow in darkness
An unexplainable Beauty

~nasreen

A SUMMER'S DAY

By the Pond I sat
Throwing Pebbles in the still Water
Marvelling at the Lotus Blossoms

~nasreen

FORGOTTEN LOVE

Bluebells and Roses
Daisies and Posies

Forgotten blossoms on my pedestal
Left Memories of a broken Heart

Speechless thoughts
How can love be so unfair...?

Only yesterday we were one
And now am half

An occasional Tear on my Cheek
What is Love anyway?

A painful emotion
A broken Heart

~nasreen

SPIRITS IN THE WOODS

Deep in the Woods of Giant Oaks
A Spirit World dwells
Saving the Trees from destruction

~nasreen

(World Environment Day 2022)

THE SECRET ROMANCE

Down by the River a hidden Tree
The secret place for their Romance
Under the Moonlight he would sing his Love symphonies

~nasreen

DANCE WITH ME

A Saturday night romance
Tango got their grips until he kissed
He had lured her into the Lovers Web

~nasreen

RHYTHMS OF THE SOUL

A lonely Man on a Street
His Guitar the only companion
Playing Rhythms from his Soul
Every Heartbeat playing a note
The Strings moving faster and faster
Suddenly a crowd gathers to the sound of his Music
Showering him with Pennies
And loud applause

~nasreen

THE WAVES

Standing as if liberated on the Sandy Beach
Was it happiness or sadness bringing me here?

As I watch the Waves rolling in towards me
My Spine shivers

A magnitude of problems I left behind
We were never meant to be

A cold Winter's night
He threw me out on the Footpath

Now left in solitude
To burn in my grievances

~nasreen

MISTY MORNING

A Strange feeling over the Bridge
Mist so thick I could not see beyond

Strange voices calling out my name
A creepy feeling engulfs me

Swallowing with difficulty
Even though a gentle Breeze surrounds me

Shivers running down my Spine
As I turn back something grasps my Feet

I seem to be falling endlessly
A Dark Tunnel is all I can see

I scream relentlessly
Not a Soul in sight

Hello...! Can anyone hear me...!?
Helloooooo!!!???

As I fall and hit my Head
Ouch!?? Am awake and laying on the Floor

Looking around I seem to have fallen from my Bed

Ohhh...!? Just a bad dream...Am glad!

~nasreen

LONDON'S DARKNESS

Empty Streets of London
Darkness befell and not a Soul in sight
The Bubonic plague had overtaken

~nasreen

INNOCENCE

An innocent Girl Child's melting SMILE
Winning my Heart instantly
An Orphan but scarred to her Soul

Life surely had let her down
In an Orphanage she grew up
Betrayed at such a young age

Invisible countless scars
Wherever I touch her she winces
So tiny but wounded beneath her White Skin

Ohhh sweet Child
Let faith embrace you for now
For I do not know what your future beholds
~nasreen

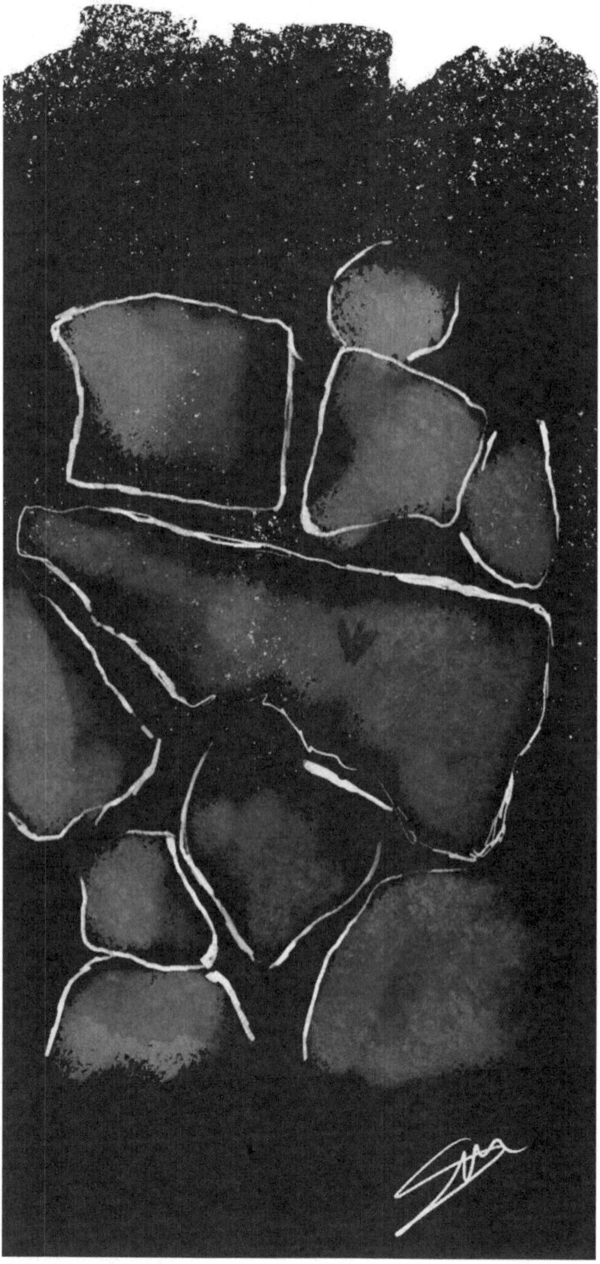

LIFE IN CRACKS

A rainy day on the Footpath
Noticing the unthinkable under my Soles
Life blossoming in cracks

~nasreen

THE SILKEN HAT

Year 1817
Women of old, adorned in beautiful Gowns and Hats
One fine Maiden, her name Emily

Left Memories in her old House
Once a hustle and bustle of activities

Now all broken down
Leaving a Tale behind

The Story of the Floral Hat
Picked by passers by

Flowers sewn out of Satin Ribbons on Silk
Stitched on the sides

A beautiful piece
Am left searching for answers

~nasreen

WHISPERING SHADOWS

Weeping Willows hanging over a Pond
Memories of a lost past
These Canopies whispering an old Tale

~nasreen

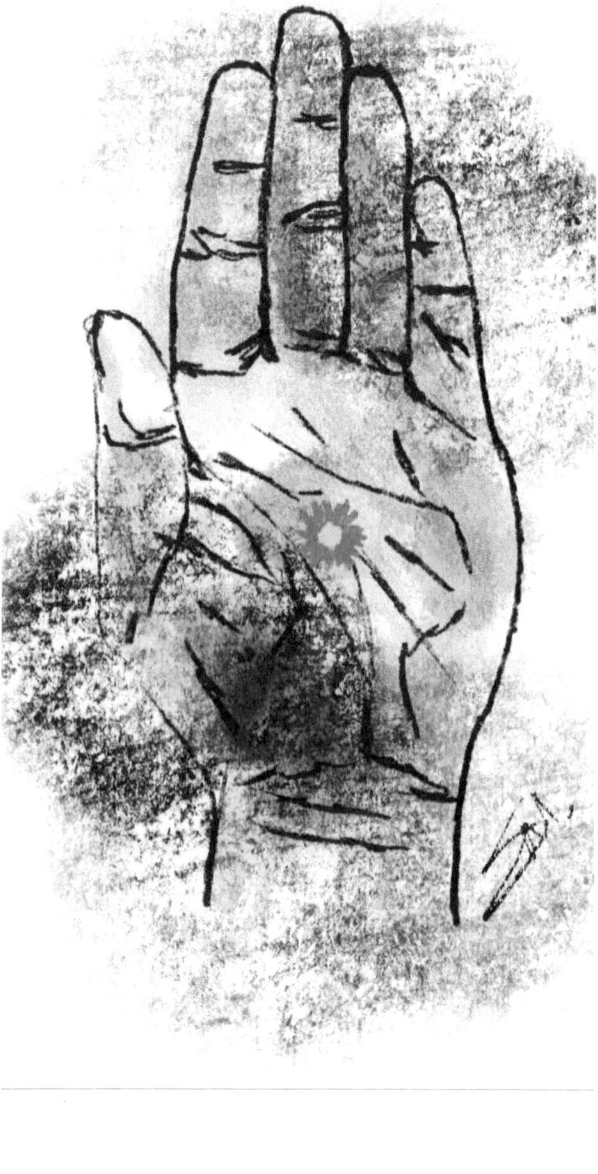

HANDS

His old Hands telling a Story
Torn Skin and broken Nails
Years of hard work left him worthless

~nasreen

ENIGMATIC WOMAN

Baffling behaviour overtaking her thoughts
Making many Heads turn
Disappearing into the Dark Alleys at Midnight

~nasreen

ANGELA

Swish swash the Brushes
Moving on the Canvas
Now let me think 'he said'...

His Mind running Wild
Naughty thoughts overwhelming his imagination

Beauty lies in the Eyes of the beholder
'Ohh My Precious'...

'My sweet Angela'
'How I miss you'...

Your caresses'
'Your gentle touches'

'You make me explode with intimacy'
'Ohh My Angela'

'My sweet candied Angela'
'She left me for another'...

His painting qualities putting his thoughts into a picture
'My sweet Kisses'

Deeply engrossed in his erotic thoughts
Dreaming of making love to her

He portrays a nude beauty
Sweet Angela

More beautiful than reality
If only....!?

Yess... If only this dream would be reality
Painting on her fancy

Suddenly a giggle
Laughter coming from nowhere

'Hello my darling....I missed you too
Holding him by the Collar

Pulling him towards her
A deep passionate Kiss it was

Uncontrollable hunger to have her
What a beauty she is...!?

Her Bossom making him tingle
'At last I found my Woman'

His thoughts running Wild
Planting Kisses all over the Canvas painting

Slapping himself gently
Wake up...! Wake up...! Diverting his Mind

Was this just a Dream...!?
'Sweet Angela speak to me'

Silence once again creeps in...
Leaving a Heartache for his sweet love

~nasreen

THE EMPTY BENCH

In the Dark, a lonely Bench
She once sat there counting the Stars
Now even the Moon is sad

~nasreen

IMPRINTS

Marking their imprints on the Sand

As a gesture of True Love

Suddenly the Waves wash away the fond memories

~nasreen

LIFE IN A BUBBLE

Tiny as it is...Life in a Bubble
The Ant pushing a Dew Drop home
For Water is Life

~nasreen

SHATTERED DREAMS

Sitting forlorn a fine Maiden
Lost in her own World

The Water Pot a symbol of her daily chores
Life has it's miseries

Poor and desolate
Tirelessly collecting Water from the River

Earning a mere few Pennies in a day
Dreaming of an unforseen future

Illiterate and Broken
Made to believe her worth is just a house help

Invisible Chains at her Ankles
Male dominance a sign of Patriarchy

~nasreen

LOVE

In the Realms of Darkness
LOVE lied once more
A One Night stand

~nasreen

ACKNOWLEDGEMENT

My sincerest thanks to Saher Malik, my Daughter, for her patience, time and effort in drawing the illustrations and helping me compile "MOONLIGHT SILENCE"

And also creating the cover design.

My sincerest thanks also goes to Bluerose Publishers, New Delhi, India, for spending their valuable time on compiling the final manuscript.